ISBN 978-0-06-331284-5

23 24 25 26 27 RTLO 10 9 8 7 6 5 4 3 2 1
Originally published in Great Britain 2023 by Farshore
First US edition, 2023

ONLINE SAFETY FOR YOUNGER FANS

Spending time online is great fun! Here are a few simple rules to help younger fans stay safe and keep the internet a great place to spend time:
- Never give out your real name – don't use it as your username.
- Never give out any of your personal details.
- Never tell anybody which school you go to or how old you are.
- Never tell anybody your password except a parent or a guardian.
- Be aware that you must be 13 or over to create an account on many sites. Always check the site policy and ask a parent or guardian for permission before registering.
- Always tell a parent or guardian if something is worrying you.

Stay safe online. Any website addresses listed in this book are correct at the time of going to print. However, Farshore is not responsible for content hosted by third parties. Please be aware that online content can be subject to change and websites can contain content that is unsuitable for children. We advise that all children are supervised when using the internet.

ADOPT ME!

PERFECT PETS
JOURNAL

HARPER
An Imprint of HarperCollinsPublishers

CONTENTS

WELCOME!

Welcome to Adoption Island! If you love exploring and taking care of the cutest pets, you've come to the right place! In Adopt Me, you can collect and trade pets to look after, dress up and play with. You can also meet with friends and complete challenges and events together. There is so much to do!

My name is: Stas.....................

My pet's name is: mushu..............

ALL ABOUT PETS

In Adopt Me, it's all about the pets! You'll meet lots of different creatures in the game. Here are a few things you need to know about your new friends.

Most pets hatch from eggs which you can find at the nursery. As you take care of your pets – feeding them, playing with them and teaching them tricks – they age up. Sometimes you can get new pets from playing events or by logging in regularly.

When you collect four of the same fully grown pet, you can go to the Neon Cave to merge their spirits into one very extraordinary Neon pet!

Pets come in five levels of rarity:

COMMON - most likely when hatching an egg
UNCOMMON
RARE
ULTRA-RARE
LEGENDARY - least likely when hatching an egg

I love pets that are:

- ☑ **Common**
- ☐ **Uncommon**
- ☐ **Rare**
- ☐ **Ultra-Rare**
- ☑ **Legendary**
- ☐ **Neon**
- ☑ **Mega Neon**
- ☐ **Furry**
- ☐ **Slimy**

- ☑ **Scaly**
- ☐ **Silly**
- ☐ **Sleepy**
- ☐ **Bouncy**
- ☑ **Winged**

ADOPTION ISLAND

You can reach Adoption Island through a portal from the Neighborhood. You'll find buildings, shops and places to play. Whether you're working to complete a task to age your pet or meet up with friends, there are many different places to explore!

THE SCHOOL

There are many rooms in the School, including a classroom, a pet room, a library and a computer room. Take your pet here to learn new tricks like sitting, dancing or rolling over.

PLAYGROUND

The Playground has swings, trampolines, a seesaw, a climbing frame and a slide. Your pet shows off their tricks by racing through the tunnel or weaving in and out of the poles.

TOP TIP: If you walk around and explore, you may stumble across a new building or an area you haven't been to before!

CAMPSITE

You'll find the Campsite in the mountain valley. There is a big campfire to sit around, with free marshmallows to roast. You can also snuggle up in one of the cozy tents to replenish your energy.

PIZZA SHOP

At the Pizza Shop, you can order pizza, or make some yourself by rolling out the dough and adding as many toppings as you like. You can also find the jukebox to play different music.

SALON

Visit the bright pink Salon to give your pet a new look! There are pet-friendly dyes so you can change the color of your pal. You can even grab a free donut while you wait.

HOME SWEET HOME

When you log in to the game you will spawn in your house. It is yours to decorate with cool furniture and upgrade the wallpaper and flooring – and a place to raise all your pets. Have a stroll around the Neighborhood and find your dream home!

TINY HOME

All players start out with this compact house. There is just enough space to give you and your pet somewhere to sit, sleep and shower!

TOP TIP: You can't enter a house while equipped with a vehicle – this includes roller skates!

FAMILY HOME

An upgrade from your tiny house – this one has a second floor, so a bit more space to stretch your decorating skills!

ECO HOUSE

The Eco Natural Earth House is an eye-popping find! With flowers and vines, this house really connects with the outdoors. And the triangular windows make this really unique.

TOP TIP: All houses, except Premium Plots, can be found in the Neighborhood.

ROYAL PALACE

This magnificent house has a very grand exterior, with a large porch, trees, towers and a balcony. You will need to have saved up plenty of Adopt Me Bucks for this royal residence.

What does your dream home look like? Draw it in the space below!

COMMON
PETS

MY FIRST PET

When you start playing Adopt Me, you can collect a free egg at the nursery. This egg will eventually transform into a dog or a cat. These are both Common pets.

TOP TIP: By taking care of your pet, you earn Adopt Me Bucks. This in-game currency can be used to buy toys and accessories for your pet – or you can spend it on new eggs in the nursery to hatch more pets!

My first pet is: a cat

I named it: Kitty

Its favorite outfit is: the silly one

Its favorite things to eat are:
cinnamon rolls

Its cutest trick is:
Joyfull

These are the places we like to play:
campsite

Once you adopt a pet, they're yours and will follow you around from your home in the Neighborhood through the tunnel to Adoption Island and back again! They'll be your pet forever, or until you trade them to other players.

MY TRADES

Think about trading and circle the answer below!

Did you trade your starter pet?
Yes / No

Would you trade your starter pet for one of these pets or items?

Bullfrog (Common)
Yes / Maybe / No way!

Chick (Common)
Yes / Maybe / No way!

Walrus (Common)
Yes / Maybe / No way!

Fennec Fox (Uncommon)
Yes / Maybe / No way!

Hyperspeed Potion (Common)
Yes / Maybe / No way!

Butterfly Roller Skates (Rare)
Yes / Maybe / No way!

Grappling Hook (Ultra-Rare)
Yes / Maybe / No way!

DOG

TOP FACTS

- Hatches from a Starter Egg or a Retired Egg

- As a Neon, glows light blue on its paws, tail and ears

I HAVE ADOPTED THIS PET!

Its name is: Perro.....................

○ Dog ⊘ Neon Dog ○ Mega Neon Dog

I adopted it on this date: August 20th 2023

○ Hatched ⊘ Traded

This is what I like best about the Dog:
its blue

This is my Dog's favorite trick:
JUMP

CAT

TOP FACTS

- Hatches from a Starter Egg or a Retired Egg
- As a Neon, glows light pink on its paws, ears, whiskers and nose

I HAVE ADOPTED THIS PET!

Its name is: carl

○ Cat   ○ Neon Cat   ✓ Mega Neon Cat

I adopted it on this date: august 16 2023

○ Hatched   ✓ Traded

This is what I like best about the Cat:

its a mega

This is what my Cat likes to wear:

glasses

BULLFROG

TOP FACTS

- Hatches from a Woodland Egg

- As a Neon, glows bright purple from its underbelly

I HAVE ADOPTED THIS PET!

Its name is: . . . .

○ Bullfrog ○ Neon Bullfrog
○ Mega Neon Bullfrog

I adopted it on this date: . . . .

○ Hatched ○ Traded

This is what I like best about the Bullfrog:

. . . .

This is what my Bullfrog likes to eat:

. . . .

OTTER

TOP FACTS

- Hatches from a Retired Egg

- As a Neon, glows bright yellow on its feet, tail, nose and ears

I HAVE ADOPTED THIS PET!

Its name is: . . . .

◯ Otter ◯ Neon Otter ◯ Mega Neon Otter

I adopted it on this date: . . . .

◯ Hatched ◯ Traded

This is what I like best about the Otter:

. . . .

This is where my Otter likes to play:

. . . .

MOUSE

TOP FACTS

- Hatches from a Pet Egg or a Cracked Egg

- As a Neon, glows blue on its feet, nose and inner ears

I HAVE ADOPTED THIS PET!

Its name is: . . . .

○ Mouse ○ Neon Mouse
○ Mega Neon Mouse

I adopted it on this date: . . . .

○ Hatched ○ Traded

This is what I like best about the Mouse:

. . . .

This is what my Mouse likes to wear:

. . . .

ANT

TOP FACTS

- Hatches from a Pet Egg or a Cracked Egg

- As a Neon, glows yellow on its antennae, chest and back

I HAVE ADOPTED THIS PET!

Its name is: . . . .

○ Ant ○ Neon Ant ○ Mega Neon Ant

I adopted it on this date: . . . .

○ Hatched ○ Traded

This is what I like best about the Ant:

. . . .

This is what my Ant likes to eat:

. . . .

MORE COMMON PETS LOG

TOP TIP: It's OK if you don't have all these pets. You can always come back and write in more information when you adopt new pets!

I HAVE THESE COMMON PETS:

Bandicoot:

Name: . . . .
- ○ Bandicoot ○ Neon Bandicoot
- ○ Mega Neon Bandicoot
- ○ Hatched: . . . . (Date)
- ○ Traded: . . . . (Date)

Buffalo:

Name: . . . .
- ○ Buffalo ○ Neon Buffalo
- ○ Mega Neon Buffalo
- ○ Hatched: . . . . (Date)
- ○ Traded: . . . . (Date)

Chicken:

Name: . . . .

○ Chicken ○ Neon Chicken

○ Mega Neon Chicken

○ Hatched: . . . . (Date)

○ Traded: . . . . (Date)

Dugong:

Name: . . . .

○ Dugong ○ Neon Dugong

○ Mega Neon Dugong

○ Hatched: . . . . (Date)

○ Traded: . . . . (Date)

Ground Sloth:

Name: . . . .

○ Ground Sloth ○ Neon Ground Sloth

○ Mega Neon Ground Sloth

○ Hatched: . . . . (Date)

○ Traded: . . . . (Date)

Robin:

Name: . . . .

○ Robin ○ Neon Robin

○ Mega Neon Robin

○ Hatched: . . . . (Date)

○ Traded: . . . . (Date)

Sado Mole:

Name: . . . .

◯ Sado Mole ◯ Neon Sado Mole
◯ Mega Neon Sado Mole
◯ Hatched: . . . . (Date)
◯ Traded: . . . . (Date)

Stingray:

Name: . . . .

◯ Stingray ◯ Neon Stingray
◯ Mega Neon Stingray
◯ Hatched: . . . . (Date)
◯ Traded: . . . . (Date)

Tasmanian Tiger:

Name: . . . .

◯ Tasmanian Tiger ◯ Neon Tasmanian Tiger
◯ Mega Neon Tasmanian Tiger
◯ Hatched: . . . . (Date)
◯ Traded: . . . . (Date)

Walrus:

Name: . . . .

◯ Walrus ◯ Neon Walrus
◯ Mega Neon Walrus
◯ Hatched: . . . . (Date)
◯ Traded: . . . . (Date)

COPY CAT

Copy the cat using the grid as a guide. Don't forget to color it in!

DOG DRESSING

How would you like to dress your dog today?
Draw four new outfits for your dog.

TOP TIPS – STARTING OUT

When you first start to play, you may want to spend some time building your collection of pets. There are so many different cute animals in the game – and new ones are added all the time!

1 COLLECT EGGS FROM THE NURSERY

Many pets can be hatched from eggs, which you can buy from the Nursery. The cheapest egg is the Cracked Egg, so these are a good option at the beginning. Plus, Cracked Eggs can hatch into some very cool pets!

2 USE THE GUMBALL MACHINE

At the Gumball Machine, you can buy themed eggs, like a Farm Egg or Safari Egg. These are often limited, meaning that they're only available for a certain period of time. You might get a very unique pet from the Gumball Machine!

3 JOIN IN DURING EVENTS

Some pets can be earned by completing challenges during Events, which might be themed around seasons or holidays, like Easter or Halloween. Keep a careful eye out for events, because they only happen for a limited time.

4 TAKE CARE OF YOUR EGGS TO HATCH THEM

Each egg takes a certain number of tasks to hatch. You might need to give them food or water, or take them to the Playground. The rarer the egg you have, the more tasks you'll need to complete before it hatches.

UNCOMMON PETS

CAMEL

TOP FACTS

- Hatches from a Pet Egg, a Cracked Egg or a Retired Egg

- As a Neon, glows bright pink on its body and the insides of its ears

I HAVE ADOPTED THIS PET!

Its name is: . . . .

○ Camel ○ Neon Camel
○ Mega Neon Camel

I adopted it on this date: . . . .

○ Hatched ○ Traded

This is what I like best about the Camel:

. . . .

This is my Camel's favorite trick:

. . . .

CRAB

TOP FACTS

- Hatches from an Ocean Egg

- As a Neon, glows bright pink on its underbelly and pincers

I HAVE ADOPTED THIS PET!

Its name is: . . . .

○ Crab ○ Neon Crab ○ Mega Neon Crab

I adopted it on this date: . . . .

○ Hatched ○ Traded

This is what I like best about the Crab:

This is what my Crab likes to wear:

. . . .

FENNEC FOX

TOP FACTS

- Hatches from a Retired Egg

- As a Neon, glows teal on its ears, nose and paws – and on the very tip of its tail

I HAVE ADOPTED THIS PET!

Its name is: . . . .

○ Fennec Fox   ○ Neon Fennec Fox
○ Mega Neon Fennec Fox

I adopted it on this date: . . . .

○ Hatched   ○ Traded

This is what I like best about the Fennec Fox:

. . . .

This is where my Fennec Fox likes to play:

. . . .

RED CARDINAL

TOP FACTS

- Hatches from a Woodland Egg

- As a Neon, glows light blue on the ends of its wings and tail feather

I HAVE ADOPTED THIS PET!

Its name is: . . . .

◯ Red Cardinal ◯ Neon Red Cardinal
◯ Mega Neon Red Cardinal

I adopted it on this date: . . . .

◯ Hatched ◯ Traded

This is what I like best about the Red Cardinal:

. . . .

This is what my Red Cardinal likes to eat:

. . . .

SILLY DUCK

TOP FACTS

- Hatches from a Farm Egg

- As a Neon, glows bright green on its head and neck

I HAVE ADOPTED THIS PET!

Its name is: . . . .

○ Silly Duck ○ Neon Silly Duck
○ Mega Neon Silly Duck

I adopted it on this date: . . . .

○ Hatched ○ Traded

This is what I like best about the Silly Duck:

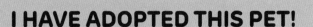

This is what my Silly Duck likes to wear:

. . . .

STEGOSAURUS

TOP FACTS

- Hatches from a Fossil Egg

- As a Neon, glows amber on its feet and the plates along its back

I HAVE ADOPTED THIS PET!

Its name is: . . . .

○ Stegosaurus ○ Neon Stegosaurus
○ Mega Neon Stegosaurus

I adopted it on this date: . . . .

○ Hatched ○ Traded

This is what I like best about the Stegosaurus:

. . . .

This is where my Stegosaurus likes to play:

. . . .

MORE UNCOMMON PETS LOG

TOP TIP: It's OK if you don't have all these pets. You can always come back and write in more information when you adopt new pets!

I HAVE THESE UNCOMMON PETS:

Black Panther:

Name: . . . .

○ Black Panther ○ Neon Black Panther

○ Mega Neon Black Panther

○ Hatched: . . . . (Date)

○ Traded: . . . . (Date)

Dingo:

Name: . . . .

○ Dingo ○ Neon Dingo

○ Mega Neon Dingo

○ Hatched: . . . . (Date)

○ Traded: . . . . (Date)

Dolphin:

Name: . . . .

○ **Dolphin** ○ **Neon Dolphin**
○ **Mega Neon Dolphin**
○ **Hatched:** . . . . **(Date)**
○ **Traded:** . . . . **(Date)**

Ermine:

Name: . . . .

○ **Ermine** ○ **Neon Ermine**
○ **Mega Neon Ermine**
○ **Hatched:** . . . . **(Date)**
○ **Traded:** . . . . **(Date)**

Glyptodon:

Name: . . . .

○ **Glyptodon** ○ **Neon Glyptodon**
○ **Mega Neon Glyptodon**
○ **Hatched:** . . . . **(Date)**
○ **Traded:** . . . . **(Date)**

Meerkat:

Name: . . . .

○ **Meerkat** ○ **Neon Meerkat**
○ **Mega Neon Meerkat**
○ **Hatched:** . . . . **(Date)**
○ **Traded:** . . . . **(Date)**

Puma:

Name: . . . .

◯ Puma ◯ Neon Puma

◯ Mega Neon Puma

◯ Hatched: . . . .(Date)

◯ Traded: . . . .(Date)

Rhino Beetle:

Name: . . . .

◯ Rhino Beetle ◯ Neon Rhino Beetle

◯ Mega Neon Rhino Beetle

◯ Hatched: . . . .(Date)

◯ Traded: . . . .(Date)

Slug:

Name: . . . .

◯ Slug ◯ Neon Slug

◯ Mega Neon Slug

◯ Hatched: . . . .(Date)

◯ Traded: . . . .(Date)

Tanuki:

Name: . . . .

◯ Tanuki ◯ Neon Tanuki

◯ Mega Neon Tanuki

◯ Hatched: . . . .(Date)

◯ Traded: . . . .(Date)

ROCK AND ROLL

Some pets are furry, some pets are scaly ... and some are rock stars! The Pet Rock was introduced on April Fools' Day. Its tricks include stay, sit still and play dead!

How would you like to decorate these pet rocks? You can add eyes, a mouth and any accessories you can dream up!

SILLY DUCK JOKES

The Silly Duck is an Uncommon pet that is known for its silly movement – swaying back and forth and bobbing its head up and down! Now it's your turn to be silly! See if you can get your friends to quack up with these great duck jokes!

Q. When do ducks get up in the morning?

A. At the quack of dawn!

Q. How did the duck egg cross the road?

A. It scrambled across!

Q. Why do ducks fly south for the winter?

A. Because it's too far to waddle!

Q. What do you call a duck who tries to steal something from you?

A. A robber duck!

Q. What do you say if it's raining ducks and chickens outside?

A. "That's fowl weather!"

TOP TIPS – PET CARE

When your pet first hatches, it will be a newborn. It is still a baby, and it hasn't even learned any tricks yet! But if you spend some time looking after your pet, it will soon age up to a junior, a pre-teen, a teen, a post-teen and finally fully grown!

1 LOOK FOR FREE FOOD AND BEVERAGES

Your pet will be hungry and thirsty. Most food costs Adopt Me Bucks, but you can find free food. Keep an eye out for the free marshmallows at the Campsite, free donuts at the Salon and free water and apples at the School.

2 SET UP SPACE AT HOME TO HELP YOUR PET

You can complete lots of tasks without even leaving your home if you prepare your room ahead of time. By buying a cheap crib, water bowl, food bowl and piano, you can help your pets age up when they are asleep, thirsty, hungry or bored.

3 TELEPORT BETWEEN TASKS

You can speed up moving between tasks by teleporting to some places. When you click on your backpack to see your inventory, the green plus icon will bring up a window that asks if you want to teleport to the shops.

4 HAVE FUN WITH YOUR PET!

Remember to have a great time playing with your pet! You can buy pet toys like bones and shoe toys for your dog to chase after. While most pet toys don't complete tasks, they are so much fun!

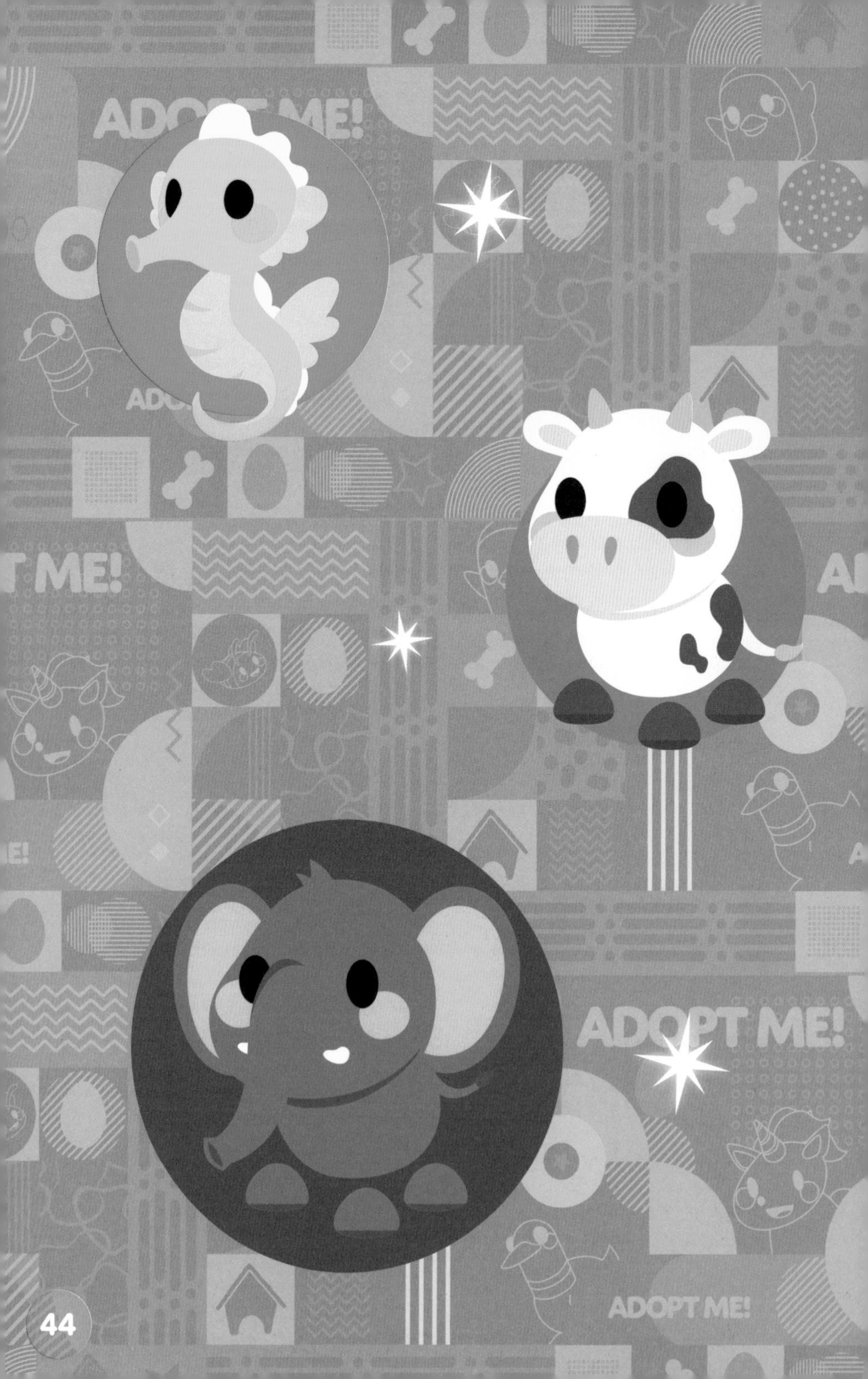
ADOPT ME!
ADOPT ME!
ADOPT ME!

RARE PETS

COW

TOP FACTS

- Hatches from a Farm Egg
- As a Neon, glows light pink on its feet, tail, ears, nose and spots

I HAVE ADOPTED THIS PET!

Its name is: . . . .

○ Cow ○ Neon Cow ○ Mega Neon Cow

I adopted it on this date: . . . .

○ Hatched ○ Traded

This is what I like best about the Cow:

. . . .

This is where my Cow likes to play:

. . . .

ELEPHANT

TOP FACTS

- Hatches from a Safari Egg

- As a Neon, glows peach on its feet, ears, tusks and the very tip of its tail

I HAVE ADOPTED THIS PET!

Its name is: . . . .

◯ Elephant ◯ Neon Elephant
◯ Mega Neon Elephant

I adopted it on this date: . . . .

◯ Hatched ◯ Traded

This is what I like best about the Elephant:

. . . .

This is what my Elephant likes to wear:

. . . .

NARWHAL

TOP FACTS

- Hatches from an Ocean Egg

- As a Neon, glows green on its back and underbelly

I HAVE ADOPTED THIS PET!

Its name is: . . . .

○ Narhwal ○ Neon Narwhal
○ Mega Neon Narwhal

I adopted it on this date: . . . .

○ Hatched ○ Traded

This is what I like best about the Narwhal:

. . . .

This is my Narwhal's favorite trick:

. . . .

RHINO

TOP FACTS

- Hatches from a Jungle Egg
- As a Neon, glows pink on its feet, ears, horn and the very tip of its tail

I HAVE ADOPTED THIS PET!

Its name is: . . . .

○ Rhino ○ Neon Rhino
○ Mega Neon Rhino

I adopted it on this date: . . . .

○ Hatched ○ Traded

This is what I like best about the Rhino:

. . . .

This is what my Rhino likes to eat:

. . . .

SEAHORSE

TOP FACTS

- Hatches from an Ocean Egg

- As a Neon, glows white on its underbelly and fins

I HAVE ADOPTED THIS PET!

Its name is: . . . .

○ Seahorse ○ Neon Seahorse
○ Mega Neon Seahorse

I adopted it on this date: . . . .

○ Hatched ○ Traded

This is what I like best about the Seahorse:

. . . .

This is what my Seahorse likes to wear:

. . . .

WOOLLY MAMMOTH

TOP FACTS

- **Hatches from a Fossil Egg**

- **As a Neon, glows light red on its feet, tail, tusks and the insides of its ears**

I HAVE ADOPTED THIS PET!

Its name is: . . . .

○ Woolly Mammoth
○ Neon Woolly Mammoth
○ Mega Neon Woolly Mammoth

I adopted it on this date: . . . .

○ Hatched ○ Traded

This is what I like best about the Woolly Mammoth:

. . . .

MORE RARE PETS LOG

TOP TIP: It's OK if you don't have all these pets. You can always come back and write in more information when you adopt new pets!

I HAVE THESE RARE PETS:

Australian Kelpie:

Name: . . . .

○ Australian Kelpie

○ Neon Australian Kelpie

○ Mega Neon Australian Kelpie

○ Hatched: . . . . (Date)

○ Traded: . . . . (Date)

Basilisk:

Name: . . . .

○ Basilisk   ○ Neon Basilisk

○ Mega Neon Basilisk

○ Hatched: . . . . (Date)

○ Traded: . . . . (Date)

Dilophosaurus:

Name: . . . .

⭘ Dilophosaurus ⭘ Neon Dilophosaurus

⭘ Mega Neon Dilophosaurus

⭘ Hatched: . . . . (Date)

⭘ Traded: . . . . (Date)

Ghost Wolf:

Name: . . . .

⭘ Ghost Wolf ⭘ Neon Ghost Wolf

⭘ Mega Neon Ghost Wolf

⭘ Hatched: . . . . (Date)

⭘ Traded: . . . . (Date)

Koi Carp:

Name: . . . .

⭘ Koi Carp ⭘ Neon Koi Carp

⭘ Mega Neon Koi Carp

⭘ Hatched: . . . . (Date)

⭘ Traded: . . . . (Date)

Lunar Tiger:

Name: . . . .

⭘ Lunar Tiger ⭘ Neon Lunar Tiger

⭘ Mega Neon Lunar Tiger

⭘ Hatched: . . . . (Date)

⭘ Traded: . . . . (Date)

Merhorse:

Name: . . . .

○ Merhorse ○ Neon Merhorse
○ Mega Neon Merhorse
○ Hatched: . . . . (Date)
○ Traded: . . . . (Date)

Orangutan:

Name: . . . .

○ Orangutan ○ Neon Orangutan
○ Mega Neon Orangutan
○ Hatched: . . . . (Date)
○ Traded: . . . . (Date)

Woodpecker:

Name: . . . .

○ Woodpecker ○ Neon Woodpecker
○ Mega Neon Woodpecker:
○ Hatched: . . . . (Date)
○ Traded: . . . . (Date)

Zebra:

Name: . . . .

○ Zebra ○ Neon Zebra
○ Mega Neon Zebra
○ Hatched: . . . . (Date)
○ Traded: . . . . (Date)

SASQUATCH SPOTTER

The Sasquatch is a Rare pet known for its furry body, arms and face. Only the first picture is a real Sasquatch. Spot one difference in each of the other five pictures.

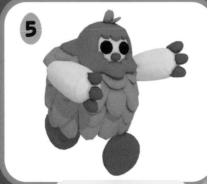

Answers on page 95

RARE PET RACE

Imagine you have four full-grown Rare pets. How quickly can you race to the Neon Cave to make a Neon pet?

HOW TO PLAY: Put your finger on the START, then trace a path, stepping ONLY on the stones with the picture of a Rare pet on them. You can go forward, backward, up or down.

START

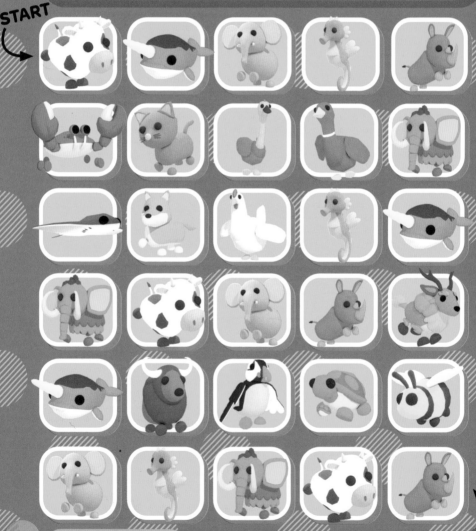

FINISH

Answers on page 95

TOP TIPS – MAKING BUCKS

Adopt Me Bucks are used to buy almost everything in the game. Luckily, there are many things you can do to earn Bucks to spend on food, toys, accessories ... and more eggs to hatch! Here are five tips for making Adopt Me Bucks:

1 COLLECT DAILY REWARDS

Every time you log in, you'll get your daily reward. Often, this is Adopt Me Bucks. It's as simple as that!

2 LOOK AFTER YOUR PET

Every time you take care of one of your pets – like feeding, bathing or healing them – you'll earn Bucks.

3 PLAY AS A BABY

You can choose to play as a baby or a grown-up. If you play as a baby, you'll get to complete tasks for yourself at the same time. You can earn twice as many Bucks!

4 CHECK YOUR DAILY TASK BOARD

Daily tasks will appear if you click on the task board on the left-hand side of the screen. You can keep up to seven tasks on this board at once, from collecting a new pet to giving a gift to another player.

5 GET A JOB

You can get a job at the Pizza Shop or the Salon on Adoption Island. Whichever job you choose, you can earn up to fifty Adopt Me Bucks a day.

ULTRA-RARE PETS

FLAMINGO

TOP FACTS

- **Hatches from a Safari Egg**
- **As a Neon, glows orange on its wings, feet and the middle of its beak**

I HAVE ADOPTED THIS PET!

Its name is: . . . .

○ Flamingo ○ Neon Flamingo
○ Mega Neon Flamingo

I adopted it on this date: . . . .

○ Hatched ○ Traded

This is what I like best about the Flamingo:

. . . .

This is what my Flamingo likes to wear:

. . . .

KOALA

TOP FACTS

- Hatches from an Aussie Egg
- As a Neon, glows light blue on its feet, nose and the insides of its ears

I HAVE ADOPTED THIS PET!

Its name is: . . . .

◯ Koala ◯ Neon Koala ◯ Mega Neon Koala

I adopted it on this date: . . . .

◯ Hatched ◯ Traded

This is what I like best about the Koala:

. . . .

This is my Koala's favorite trick:

. . . .

LION

TOP FACTS

- Hatches from a Safari Egg
- As a Neon, glows light blue on its paws, nose, ears and the very tip of its tail

I HAVE ADOPTED THIS PET!

Its name is: . . . .

○ Lion ○ Neon Lion ○ Mega Neon Lion

I adopted it on this date: . . . .

○ Hatched ○ Traded

This is what I like best about the Lion:

. . . .

This is what my Lion likes to eat:

. . . .

RED PANDA

TOP FACTS

- Hatches from a Retired Egg
- As a Neon, glows bright red on its feet, nose, ears and tail stripes

I HAVE ADOPTED THIS PET!

Its name is: . . . .

◯ Red Panda ◯ Neon Red Panda
◯ Mega Neon Red Panda

I adopted it on this date: . . . .

◯ Hatched ◯ Traded

This is what I like best about the Red Panda:

. . . .

This is where my Red Panda likes to play:

. . . .

SHIBA INU

TOP FACTS

- Hatches from a Retired Egg

- As a Neon, glows light orange on its paws, tail and the insides of its ears

I HAVE ADOPTED THIS PET!

Its name is: . . . .

○ Shiba Inu ○ Neon Shiba Inu
○ Mega Neon Shiba Inu

I adopted it on this date: . . . .

○ Hatched ○ Traded

This is what I like best about the Shiba Inu:

. . . .

This is what my Shiba Inu likes to wear:

. . . .

WYVERN

TOP FACTS

- Hatches from a Mythic Egg
- As a Neon, glows white on its wings, spikes and underbelly

I HAVE ADOPTED THIS PET!

Its name is: . . . .

○ Wyvern ○ Neon Wyvern
○ Mega Neon Wyvern

I adopted it on this date: . . . .

○ Hatched ○ Traded

This is what I like best about the Wyvern:

. . . .

This is my Wyvern's favorite trick:

. . . .

MORE ULTRA-RARE PETS LOG

TOP TIP: It's OK if you don't have all these pets. You can always come back and write in more information when you adopt new pets!

I HAVE THESE ULTRA-RARE PETS:

Arctic Fox:

Name: . . . .
- ◯ Arctic Fox
- ◯ Neon Arctic Fox
- ◯ Mega Neon Arctic Fox
- ◯ Hatched: . . . . (Date)
- ◯ Traded: . . . . (Date)

Badger:

Name: . . . .
- ◯ Badger
- ◯ Neon Badger
- ◯ Mega Neon Badger
- ◯ Hatched: . . . . (Date)
- ◯ Traded: . . . . (Date)

Corgi:

Name: . . . .

○ **Corgi** ○ **Neon Corgi**

○ **Mega Neon Corgi**

○ **Hatched:** . . . . **(Date)**

○ **Traded:** . . . . **(Date)**

Deinonychus:

Name: . . . .

○ **Deinonychus** ○ **Neon Deinonychus**

○ **Mega Neon Deinonychus**

○ **Hatched:** . . . . **(Date)**

○ **Traded:** . . . . **(Date)**

Orca:

Name: . . . .

○ **Orca** ○ **Neon Orca**

○ **Mega Neon Orca**

○ **Hatched:** . . . . **(Date)**

○ **Traded:** . . . . **(Date)**

Pine Marten:

Name: . . . .

○ **Pine Marten** ○ **Neon Pine Marten**

○ **Mega Neon Pine Marten**

○ **Hatched:** . . . . **(Date)**

○ **Traded:** . . . . **(Date)**

Robot:

Name: . . . .

◯ **Robot** ◯ **Neon Robot**

◯ **Mega Neon Robot**

◯ **Hatched:** . . . . **(Date)**

◯ **Traded:** . . . . **(Date)**

Sloth:

Name: . . . .

◯ **Sloth** ◯ **Neon Sloth**

◯ **Mega Neon Sloth**

◯ **Hatched:** . . . . **(Date)**

◯ **Traded:** . . . . **(Date)**

Space Whale:

Name: . . . .

◯ **Space Whale** ◯ **Neon Space Whale**

◯ **Mega Neon Space Whale**

◯ **Hatched:** . . . . **(Date)**

◯ **Traded:** . . . . **(Date)**

Zombie Wolf:

Name: . . . .

◯ **Zombie Wolf** ◯ **Neon Zombie Wolf**

◯ **Mega Neon Zombie Wolf**

◯ **Hatched:** . . . . **(Date)**

◯ **Traded:** . . . . **(Date)**

WYVERN'S WORD SEARCH

Can you help the Wyvern find the names of these other Ultra-Rare pets? Names read across, down and diagonally. Look carefully – just like Ultra-Rare pets, they might be tricky to find!

U	D	G	J	B	E	E	A	T	U	P	G	B	B	G
L	U	H	K	C	H	T	A	E	P	E	R	M	H	A
N	A	C	U	O	T	O	L	F	I	N	C	A	I	O
I	G	J	N	E	O	A	D	M	J	G	F	L	U	D
H	H	O	C	M	L	R	O	F	R	U	E	N	S	K
P	I	T	R	B	S	T	K	S	A	I	F	T	P	D
L	H	S	E	K	O	A	L	A	H	N	N	Y	L	A
O	S	J	F	P	R	T	M	I	E	R	P	E	I	D
D	I	T	N	I	F	F	U	P	C	O	L	K	O	N
R	F	W	H	K	J	O	J	B	U	B	E	R	G	A
A	R	P	C	A	P	Y	E	T	I	O	T	U	F	P
K	A	S	H	I	B	A	I	N	U	T	C	T	G	D
S	T	H	K	C	O	G	N	I	M	A	L	F	S	E
O	S	V	I	D	C	E	H	G	G	K	C	H	N	R

- [ ] Bee
- [ ] Turkey
- [ ] Yeti
- [ ] Flamingo
- [ ] Starfish
- [ ] Penguin
- [ ] Puffin
- [ ] Robot
- [ ] Red Panda
- [ ] Shiba Inu
- [ ] Toucan
- [ ] Sloth
- [ ] Koala
- [ ] Lamb
- [ ] Lion

Answers on page 95

ULTRA-RARE CHALLENGE

Challenge a friend to these true or false questions to see who knows more about Ultra-Rare pets!

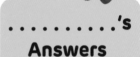

	. . . .'s Answers	. . . .'s Answers
1 Toucans hatch from Jungle Eggs.	TRUE FALSE	TRUE FALSE
2 Bees cannot be hatched, but they can be tamed with Honey.	TRUE FALSE	TRUE FALSE
3 A Flamingo grows extra wings when fed a Fly Potion.	TRUE FALSE	TRUE FALSE
4 You can make a Neon Puffin with just three Puffins.	TRUE FALSE	TRUE FALSE
5 Trapdoor Snails are unable to wear any shoe accessories.	TRUE FALSE	TRUE FALSE

Answers on page 95

TOP TIPS – FUN WITH FRIENDS

You can play Adopt Me on your own, but you can also meet up with your friends. Once you add someone as a friend in the game, you will be able to send them messages or interact with their pets.*

1 BUILD TOGETHER

Your friends can help you design and decorate your home! When you select the Build With Friends furniture stand, you can set a budget for another player to edit your house.

2 HOST A FASHION SHOW

You and your friends can choose lots of great clothes and accessories so that you're wearing matching outfits. Or even better: dress your favorite pets up to match as well!

3 CHALLENGE EACH OTHER TO OBBIES

Which of you will be the first to complete obstacle courses? The Obbies Building is at the Playground behind the slide. You'll have to run, dodge and jump to make it through each course. Start out with Mini World, and see who can finish quickest without falling in the water!

4 TAKE A HOT AIR BALLOON RIDE TOGETHER

When you jump in the Hot Air Balloon by the bridge, Captain Arg will fly you and your friends to the Sky Castle. It costs five Bucks to hire, but once you have paid, your friends can come along for free – so it's perfect for taking turns!

*Only add friends you know in real life. Check online safety advice on page 2 for further information.

LEGENDARY PETS

GIRAFFE

TOP FACTS

- Hatches from a Safari Egg
- As a Neon, glows light yellow on its spots, hooves and the insides of its ears

I HAVE ADOPTED THIS PET!

Its name is: . . . .

○ Giraffe ○ Neon Giraffe
○ Mega Neon Giraffe

I adopted it on this date: . . . .

○ Hatched ○ Traded

This is what I like best about the Giraffe:

. . . .

This is where my Giraffe likes to play:

. . . .

DRAGON

TOP FACTS

- **Hatches from a Retired Egg**
- **As a Neon, glows white on its wings, horns, hooves and fangs**

I HAVE ADOPTED THIS PET!

Its name is: . . . .

○ **Dragon** ○ **Neon Dragon**
○ **Mega Neon Dragon**

I adopted it on this date: . . . .

○ **Hatched** ○ **Traded**

This is what I like best about the Dragon:

. . . .

This is what my Dragon likes to wear:

. . . .

FALLOW DEER

TOP FACTS

- Hatches from a Woodland Egg
- As a Neon, glows green on its spots, underbelly and around its eyes

I HAVE ADOPTED THIS PET!

Its name is: . . . .

◯ Fallow Deer ◯ Neon Fallow Deer
◯ Mega Neon Fallow Deer

I adopted it on this date: . . . .

◯ Hatched ◯ Traded

This is what I like best about the Fallow Deer:

. . . .

This is what my Fallow Deer likes to eat:

. . . .

KANGAROO

TOP FACTS

- Hatches from an Aussie Egg

- As a Neon, glows pale yellow on its feet, nose, tail and the insides of its ears

I HAVE ADOPTED THIS PET!

Its name is: . . . .

○ Kangaroo ○ Neon Kangaroo
○ Mega Neon Kangaroo

I adopted it on this date: . . . .

○ Hatched ○ Traded

This is what I like best about the Kangaroo:

. . . .

This is my Kangaroo's favorite trick:

. . . .

OCTOPUS

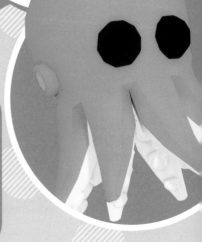

TOP FACTS

- Hatches from an Ocean Egg
- As a Neon, glows yellow on its tentacles and inside its ears

I HAVE ADOPTED THIS PET!

Its name is: . . . .

○ Octopus ○ Neon Octopus
○ Mega Neon Octopus

I adopted it on this date: . . . .

○ Hatched ○ Traded

This is what I like best about the Octopus:

. . . .

This is where my Octopus likes to play:

. . . .

UNICORN

TOP FACTS

- Hatches from an Retired Egg

- As a Neon, glows pink on its hooves, mane and tail

I HAVE ADOPTED THIS PET!

Its name is: . . . .

○ Unicorn ○ Neon Unicorn
○ Mega Neon Unicorn

I adopted it on this date: . . . .

○ Hatched ○ Traded

This is what I like best about the Unicorn:

. . . .

This is what my Unicorn likes to wear:

. . . .

MORE LEGENDARY PETS LOG

TOP TIP: It's OK if you don't have all these pets. You can always come back and write in more information when you adopt new pets!

I HAVE THESE LEGENDARY PETS:

Arctic Reindeer:

Name: . . . .

○ Arctic Reindeer

○ Neon Arctic Reindeer

○ Mega Neon Arctic Reindeer

○ Hatched: . . . . (Date)

○ Traded: . . . . (Date)

Crow:

Name: . . . .

○ Crow

○ Neon Crow

○ Mega Neon Crow

○ Hatched: . . . . (Date)

○ Traded: . . . . (Date)

Dragonfly:

Name: . . . .

◯ Dragonfly ◯ Neon Dragonfly

◯ Mega Neon Dragonfly

◯ Hatched: . . . . (Date)

◯ Traded: . . . . (Date)

Goldhorn:

Name: . . . .

◯ Goldhorn ◯ Neon Goldhorn

◯ Mega Neon Goldhorn

◯ Hatched: . . . . (Date)

◯ Traded: . . . . (Date)

Hawk:

Name: . . . .

◯ Hawk ◯ Neon Hawk

◯ Mega Neon Hawk

◯ Hatched: . . . . (Date)

◯ Traded: . . . . (Date)

Lava Dragon:

Name: . . . .

◯ Lava Dragon ◯ Neon Lava Dragon

◯ Mega Neon Lava Dragon

◯ Hatched: . . . . (Date)

◯ Traded: . . . . (Date)

Phoenix:

Name: . . . .

◯ **Phoenix** ◯ **Neon Phoenix**

◯ **Mega Neon Phoenix**

◯ **Hatched:** . . . . **(Date)**

◯ **Traded:** . . . . **(Date)**

Squid:

Name: . . . .

◯ **Squid** ◯ **Neon Squid**

◯ **Mega Neon Squid**

◯ **Hatched:** . . . . **(Date)**

◯ **Traded:** . . . . **(Date)**

Sugar Glider:

Name: . . . .

◯ **Sugar Glider** ◯ **Neon Sugar Glider**

◯ **Mega Neon Sugar Glider**

◯ **Hatched:** . . . . **(Date)**

◯ **Traded:** . . . . **(Date)**

Winged Horse:

Name: . . . .

◯ **Winged Horse** ◯ **Neon Winged Horse**

◯ **Mega Neon Winged Horse**

◯ **Hatched:** . . . . **(Date)**

◯ **Traded:** . . . . **(Date)**

SHADOW DRAGON'S SHADOW MATCH

You'll recognize the Shadow Dragon from its skeletal appearance, glowing purple eyes and visible breath. But how quickly can you recognize these other legendary pets just by their outlines? If you get stuck, have a look back at pages 72–79.

A

B

C

D

E

F

Answers on page 95

NEON PET MATCH!

It takes four of each Legendary pet to make a Neon pet.
Find four of each pet below to go to the Neon Cave.

TOP TIPS – MAKING TRADES

Some pets are no longer available to hatch or you might be looking for a certain creature to create a Neon pet. That's where trading comes in – you can swap with other players in the game for pets you're looking for!

1 BE SAFE!

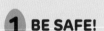

Before you can trade full-grown pets, you'll need to take the Trading License test in the Safety Hub, which you can find between the bridge and the Hat Shop. You'll have to answer a few questions to show you know how to trade safely.

2 TRY TO TRADE LIKE FOR LIKE

If you are looking for a Rare pet, you'll have a better chance of getting it by offering to trade a different Rare pet. This means they're likely to be of similar value.

3 TRADE TO COLLECT FOUR OF THE SAME PET

With four of the same pet, you can turn them into a Neon pet in the Neon Cave. If you have two or three of the same pet already, you can try and trade for a full set. This may be a lot faster than hatching enough eggs to collect them!

4 YOU DON'T *HAVE* TO TRADE!

Remember, if someone offers you something that you don't want – or that seems too good to be true – you can turn them down. You don't have to trade anything away if you don't want to!

YOUR DREAM PET

Adopt Me is full of cute, weird and wonderful pets! If you could pick any of them to be your dream pet, what would it be? Fill in all the details about your pet and imagine what you would do with it in the real world.

TYPE: . . . .

RARITY: . . . .

NAME: . . . .

LIFE STAGE: . . . .

FAVORITE FOOD: . . . .

FAVORITE ACCESSORY: . . . .

FAVORITE PLACE TO VISIT IN ADOPT ME:

. . . .

What would be your perfect day with your dream pet?

· ·

· ·

If your pet could join you at school, what would be its favorite subject, and why?

· ·

· ·

Where in the world would you take your pet on vacation?

· ·

· ·

Which other pets would be best friends with your pet?

· ·

· ·

What would your pet do if it had a job?

· ·

· ·

MY FAVORITE THINGS

There are so many things to do in Adopt Me, from looking after your pet to designing your perfect house. But are you an Adopt Me Newbie or a Legendary Leader? Tick off all the things you've done:

- ◯ **Bought ice cream**
- ◯ **Thrown a party**
- ◯ **Learned to dance**
- ◯ **Taught a pet to roll over**
- ◯ **Bounced on a trampoline**
- ◯ **Went to a pool party**
- ◯ **Drank a Hyperspeed Potion**
- ◯ **Left someone a message on a school locker**
- ◯ **Climbed to the top floor of the Toy Shop**
- ◯ **Raced a car through the Neighborhood**
- ◯ **Done a somersault on roller skates**
- ◯ **Given a friend a tour of my house**
- ◯ **Completed an Obbie**

○ Discovered a secret room

○ Used an airplane propeller to jump off a high tower

My top five favorite things to do are:

1 ....

....

2 ....

....

3 ....

....

4 ....

....

5 ....

....

WOULD YOU RATHER?

Think carefully about the choices below, and pick the one that you like best! You can also ask your friends what they would choose.

WOULD YOU RATHER HAVE...

A Dog or a Cat?

Ten Fly-A-Pet Potions or unlimited Hyperspeed Potions?

A Queen Bee or a King Penguin?

A Shadow Dragon or a Diamond Unicorn?

A Seahorse or a Narwhal?

Five thousand Adopt Me Bucks or a Robo Dog?

Three Uncommon Mega Neon Pets or one Ultra-Rare Neon Pet?

A Kitsune or an Octopus?

Five Golden Eggs to hatch or one Monkey King?

Fifty thousand Adopt Me Bucks or a Mega Neon Griffin?

SPOT THE DIFFERENCE

The pets are gathering at the Pet Shop for new toys and treats! Find ten differences between these two pictures.

Answers on page 95

GORGEOUS GIFTS

Imagine you've just received a gift box. What would you like to be inside? Use your brightest colors, and draw it below!

ANSWERS

Page 55

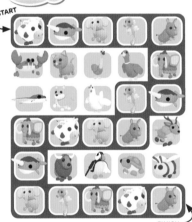

Page 56

START

FINISH

Page 69

U	D	G	J	B	E	E	A	T	U	P	G	B	B	G
L	U	H	K	C	H	T	A	E	P	E	R	M	H	A
N	A	C	U	O	T	O	K	F	I	N	C	A	I	O
I	G	J	N	E	O	A	D	I	J	G	F	L	U	D
H	H	O	C	M	L	R	O	F	R	U	E	N	S	K
P	I	T	R	B	S	T	K	S	A	I	F	T	P	D
L	H	S	E	K	O	A	L	A	H	N	N	Y	L	A
O	S	J	F	P	R	T	M	I	E	R	P	E	I	D
D	I	T	N	I	F	F	U	P	C	O	L	K	O	N
R	F	W	H	K	J	O	J	B	U	B	E	R	G	A
A	R	P	C	A	P	Y	E	T	I	O	T	U	F	P
K	A	S	H	I	B	A	I	N	U	T	C	T	G	D
S	T	H	K	C	O	G	N	I	M	A	L	F	S	E
O	S	V	I	D	C	E	H	G	G	K	C	H	N	R

Page 70

1 FALSE 2 TRUE 3 TRUE 4 FALSE 5 TRUE

Page 83

Page 84

Pages 92-93

95

Have you seen any new pets around Adoption Island? List your entire collection here!